ME.

WISC.

MICH.

N.Y. VT. N.H.

MASS.

CONN. R.I.

ILL.

IND. OHIO PA. N.J.

WVA. MD. DEL.

VA.

KY.

N.C.

TENN.

S.C.

ARKANSAS

MISS. ALA. GA.

LA.

FLA.

With Love— Christmas 1977
Betty

Matt Bradley's Arkansas

by
Donald M. Bradley, Jr.

Rose Publishing Co., Inc.
301 Louisiana
Little Rock, Ark. 72201
AC501-372-1666

PREFACE

I have learned a great deal about our state while working on this book. For one, I now realize what a great diversity Arkansas has to offer. From its many small towns to a thriving capital city, urban and rural, wilderness and metropolis, Arkansas is indeed a state of many facets.

Certainly idyllic life in the Ozarks which so frequently depicts our state is one of these. You see, Arkansans **do** eat a lot of blackeyed peas and turnip greens; but many of these same people dine occasionally on Swiss cuisine before taking in a performance of the symphony. Put another way, there is much more to our state than just country life, as you will see in the pages that follow.

Many images of Arkansas are etched in my memory, as surely as they have been recorded on film: a pot of coffee, shared with an old friend on a Buffalo River gravel bar; the intensity of an operating room during open heart surgery; a boy's hefty string of smallmouth bass and a dripping pine forest during a downpour near Crossett.

Arkansas is blessed with an abundance of natural endowments, yet I believe the state's greatest asset cannot be defined in terms of acres or tonnage, or given a dollar sign. The attribute I'm speaking of is the openness of its people, both citifed and countrified, and this is undoubtedly the greatest source of the pride I feel when I say, "Arkansas is my home."

And say, pass those blackeyed peas over this way, will you — if there are any left.

Donald M. (Matt) Bradley, Jr.

North Little Rock
September 6, 1975

Dedicated with love to my mother and father.

CONTENTS

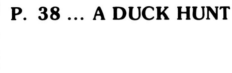

THIS IS ARKANSAS !

Rich in natural beauty, Arkansas offers a diverse geographic sampling, from steep forested slopes of the Ozark plateau in the northwest, to the flat delta country of the southeast, formed by the Arkansas and Mississippi Rivers. Twenty-three state parks offer scenic and recreational opportunities throughout the state.

Cedar Creek, Petit Jean State Park.

A concrete country club is formed in downtown Little Rock by highrise buildings, towering over Worthen Bank's fourth-story putting green (**left**). Young bankers think twice before venturing out to polish their game, however. The bank's executive offices lie directly overhead.

Noontime recreation in Romance, Arkansas, takes the form of a hot game of checkers on the porch of the general store (**above**).

In Pine Bluff, International Paper Company's 200-yard computerized "paper machine," turns steaming wood pulp into 1600 tons of milk carton stock daily.

Number one in Arkansas

FORESTS cover some 18.3 million acres, or about 55 percent of Arkansas' total land area. The forest products industry, the largest in the state, employs over 50,000 Arkansans with a payroll of a billion dollars. To ensure timber will remain a renewable resource, the forest industry practices an active replanting program. During the 1974-75 planting season, over 59 million pine and hardwood seedlings were planted throughout the state.

Logging operations in the southeast corner of the state (**right**) supply timber to Georgia Pacific's Crossett plant, the largest wood processing center in the U.S.

Music for all ears

THE 82-MEMBER ARKANSAS SYMPHONY, conducted by Kurt Klipstatter of Graz, Austria (**left**), performs 16 concerts a year, half of which are given in Little Rock. Sunday afternoon "dollar concerts" are given periodically in an effort to make the Symphony available to those unable to afford a full-price ticket and give newcomers an economical sampling.

The Symphony's 25-piece chamber orchestra is oriented to performing outside of Little Rock, while the "String Quartet", the educational arm of the Symphony, plays to 20,000 school children annually throughout the state.

The washboard and bongos her specialty, 84-year-old Mrs. Mary Major performs with Bill Worthen (left) and James Pence at the Arkansas Territorial Restoration spring arts and crafts show.

Stands of tall cypress typify Arkansas' many old river lakes (**following page**). ▶

13

LONGTIME SYMBOLS of higher education in Arkansas, "Old Main" (**left**) has overlooked the University of Arkansas campus in Fayetteville since 1875. Students (**below**) take advantage of a warm spring day and "book it" in the Greek Theater.

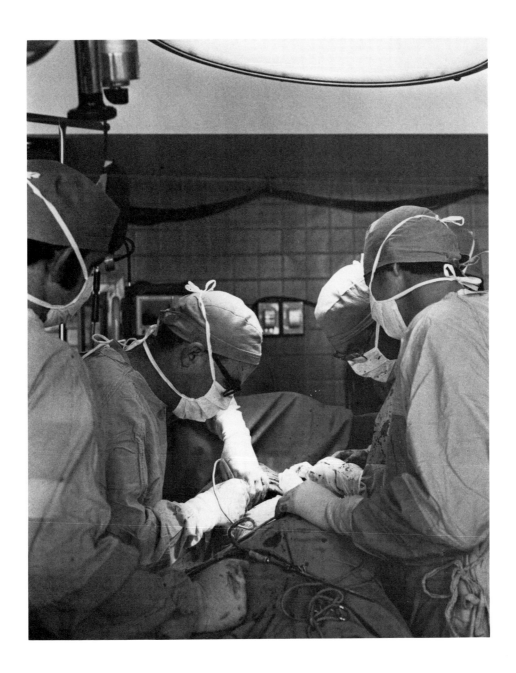

A low mortality rate has given the University of Arkansas for Medical Sciences Campus national recognition in the field of open heart surgery (**above**).

Graduating more than 100 doctors each year, the University's medical center campus houses the schools of medicine, nursing, pharmacy and health-related professions. Dr. Vern Ann Williams of Paragould, a first year-resident in pediatrics, checks on one of her young patients (**right**).

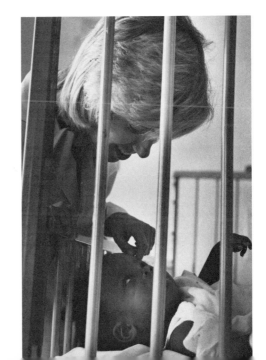

Razorback mania reigns each Fall, and an entire state reverberates with the cry of "Sooieeee Pig!" as the University of Arkansas football team takes the field in pursuit of a winning season. Over the years Razorback football fortunes have risen and fallen, but this has had little effect on the ardor of the fans, who may be described as, well... enthusiastic!

What three-year-old Jill Paige Jordan lacks in volume, she makes up in animation (**left**), as she calls the Hogs along with 54,000 other fans in Little Rock's War Memorial Stadium.

At home in a land of giants, "Lil Ike" (Phil Smith) of West Memphis (**left**) keeps a close eye on his main man, running back Ike Forte, number 85, of the Razorbacks.

19

Saudi Arabia bound, these buses on the assembly line of Ward School Bus Manufacturing, Inc. of Conway will eventually find a home transporting Moslem pilgrims to Mecca, their Holy City. The buses will be outfitted with an oversized radiator-cooling system to combat the desert heat and the stop-and-go driving on roads crowded at pilgrimage time. Two special tanks (shown above), are incorporated in the bus' design to hold water, one for drinking and the other for washing feet.

PILGRIMS GOVERNMENT TRANSPORTATION النقل الحكومي للحجاج

WITH THE COMPLETION of the McClellan-Kerr Arkansas River Navigation System, the Arkansas River provides access to barge transportation on more than half of the inland waterways in the U.S., including the international port of New Orleans. Cities either having or planning port facilities are Fort Smith, Little Rock-North Little Rock, Pine Bluff, Ozark, Russellville and Dardanelle.

FARMER'S PLOW churns up a dusty contrast to a nearby flooded rice field near Carlisle, where rice was first introduced to the state in 1904. That 70-acre experimental crop has now expanded to 700,000 acres, and Arkansas is currently the nation's number one rice producer, and the leading exporter of rice to the nations of the world. Rice and soybeans constitute the two main crops of Arkansas' Grand Prairie (**following page**).

Skyscrapers become grain elevators upon closer inspection, as Stuttgart seemingly thursts a big city skyline over the expanse of the Grand Prairie. Stretching from Crowley's Ridge on the east to the Ozark Mountains on the west, this unique geographical area in east Arkansas was judged unsuitable for cotton farming, and as late as the turn of the century still had land available for homesteading. Now, because of the abundance of grain crops, waterfowl funneling down the Mississippi Flyway are lured to the area each winter, and Stuttgart has become appropriately known as the "Duck Hunting Capital of the World."

Picker problems (**left**) caused by a muddy field are cussed and discussed by Alto Hankins of England, Arkansas (on ground), and Richard "Bunk" Williams of Scott.

Cotton is no longer king in a state whose farmers now find other crops more profitable, such as protein-rich soybeans. Of the six million acres of farmland in Arkansas, 4.6 million are planted in soybeans. Cotton still accounts for one sixth of Arkansas' total agricultural acreage, which yields around a million bales annually.

Awaiting next year's harvest, empty cotton trailers surround almost every Arkansas gin during the winter months (**following page**). ▶

Reflections of a city are mirrored by the glass windows of the thirty-story First National Bank of Little Rock (**right**), while a stream wandering through the Caney Creek back country reflects somewhat different surroundings (**above**). This 10,000-acre wilderness in western Arkansas is established and managed for those who love a secluded forest environment. No motor vehicles are allowed, so visitors must either hike or ride horseback.

Pink Tomato Festival

EACH YEAR THE BOUNTIFUL TOMATO HARVEST of Bradley County is celebrated with the Pink Tomato Festival, held each summer in Warren. Highlights include a tomato-eating contest, parade (**right**) and the Southeast Arkansas Talent Contest, held on a flat-bed trailer under the large shade trees by the courthouse.

30

Contestants belly up for some serious tomato eatin' in Warren, Arkansas.

A sequined beauty awaits her group's turn to perform a tap dance during the Southeast Arkansas Talent Contest.

Bringing art to the people

ARKANSAS IS ONE OF THE FEW SOUTHERN STATES with a statewide "Festival of the Arts." Held each spring, the Festival features fourteen separate juried competitions and a clothesline sale (**above**), open to any Arkansas-born artist and artists residing in the state.

The Arkansas Arts Center's Artmobile (**left**), carries a traveling display to schools and small towns throughout the state, while Pine Bluff's $3 million Civic Center (**below**), houses the Southeast Arkansas Arts and Science Center, featuring exhibits, theater, lectures and workshops open to all.

Dancers take their bows (right) during a performance at the Arkansas Arts Center in Little Rock. Constructed in 1963, the Center houses a theater, five exhibition galleries and extensive educational facilities in the fields of the visual and performing arts. Arts Center activities include: exhibitions, films for adults and children, a children's theater, a neighborhood arts program, Arkansas Artists in Action program, a yearly Shakespeare film festival, visiting artist workshops and traveling seminars to cultural centers of the world, including China, Egypt and France.

To help ensure the growth of the Center, a trust fund was created by the will of former governor Winthrop Rockefeller challenging the people of Arkansas to raise money for the Arkansas Arts Center Foundation. For every dollar raised by the people of Arkansas, the trust contributes three dollars, up to $1.5 million.

Square dancers do-si-do in the city park of Lonoke, Arkansas, during a city craft fair and barbeque.

Pipeline Maze—El Dorado oil refinery.
More than 16 million barrels of oil are
pumped from the El Dorado area annually,
enough to supply the United States for only
one day.

WEALTHY IN NATURAL RESOURCES, Arkansas leads the
nation in the production of bauxite, the ore from which
aluminum is made. Found only in Saline and Pulaski counties, the ore
is mined from the surface (**lower right**) after first removing a layer of
soil called overburden. Machinery such as Reynolds Metals' dragline
"Deeper Heaper" (**top right**), can scoop up three dumptruck loads of
earth in one monstrous bite. After the ore is depleted, the area is
restored to its original contour and replanted.

Little Rock soars along with sister city North Little Rock, not only statistically (Between 1961 and 1975, total retail sales of the metropolitan area including both cities increased 375% to top one billion dollars.), but also in opportunities offered to its youth. A future farmer admires a new straw hat (**right**) during the exhibit Fantastic Images and Imaginary Worlds in the "Yellow Space Place," a special children's gallery in the Arkansas Arts Center. A frisbee throwing contest (**below**) is only one of the supervised Fourth of July activities in North Little Rock's Burns Park, the second largest municipally owned park in the U.S.

A DUCK HUNT

"**M**Y FEED CALL NEEDS A LITTLE MORE WORK," commented 14-year-old Bruce Roberts (**right**). But the ducks didn't seem to mind, at least not this day, as Bruce, father Bill Roberts and Harvey McGeorge, all of Pine Bluff, had them coming in tree-top high with landing gear extended (**above**).

Arkansas duck hunters contribute over a quarter of a million dollars annually toward the acquisition of waterfowl wetlands through their purchase of federal duck stamps.

STATE

FAIR

J UST ASK any Arkansas youngster what
helps fill the intolerably long gap
between summer's end and Halloween. It is
ice cream cones and footlong hotdogs, the
ferris wheel and the Tilt-A-Whirl, the
nickel toss and a necklace for your best girl.
It's the midway at the State Fair, and
beyond everything else, it's fun!

HOT

SPRINGS

A N AQUATIC WONDERLAND: A chief attraction of the Hot Springs area has long been its water resources. Forty-seven hotwater springs gush from the base of Hot Springs Mountain at an average temperature of 143 degrees. For years the area was considered sacred by the Indians, who would lay aside their weapons and tribal differences to bathe in the hot, healing waters. Today, the springs' output of over a million gallons daily is piped to the 18 stylish spas along Bath House Row in downtown Hot Springs.

A chain of three area lakes, Catherine, Hamilton and Ouachita, provides 70,766 acres of fertile waters for fishermen, and a paradise for water skiers, both beginner and expert (**following page**).

A haven for all ages, Hot Spring's lakes furnish a sparkling playground for the young (**below**), while the town itself has become a popular retirement community. Every squirrel along the city's cobblestoned "Promenade" (**right**) has been named by Park Q. Page, who devotes a healthy part of each day strolling along the shaded walkway, handing out peanuts on request (**left**).

Thoroughbreds stretch for the finish at Hot Spring's Oaklawn race track. Arkansas' fifty-day racing season begins early in February and lasts through the first week in April. The 1975 season saw more than 855,000 fans wager $87 million.

Boats of every size and description congregate on Lake Ouachita each summer. Completely surrounded by national forest land, the Lake provides an unspoiled wilderness-like environment with more than 970 miles of shoreline for water-sports enthusiasts. Public and state campgrounds are scattered around its shores, and for those who really desire to get away from it all, there is island camping (please bring back your trash).

MRS. THOMAS' STORE

FOR MORE THAN HALF A CENTURY, since 1918 to be exact, Mrs. Thomas' general store has served the residents of Tarry, a tiny farm community ten miles north of Star City, in southeast Arkansas. At the Thomas Grocery, credit is liberal. You see, Mrs. Lois Thomas knows all her customers quite well - and their mothers and fathers, and a good many of the grandfolk too.

No matter what is needed, likely as not it can be found in the store, from a sack of flour to a new pair of shoes and everything in between, including the town's only gas pump. Up until 1963, when Mrs. Thomas reached the mandatory government retirement age, the store housed the Tarry Post Office in one corner. "Every morning I was here by six," she explained. "Had to have the mail sorted and ready to go for the pickup from Pine Bluff."

In winter, when the weather turns foul and Mrs. Thomas' wood-burning stove is glowing red, the store becomes a favorite gathering place to swap stories and speculate on next year's crop. An old bench, its wooden surface polished by years of use, becomes a focal point, mainly because of its close proximity to the stove.

Mrs. Thomas, who will soon celebrate her 78th birthday, spends much of her time in a favorite rocker, reading or knitting. In the summer, you might catch her napping in the afternoon, behind the old post office front near the fan. But when the rickety screen door slams, announcing the arrival of a young customer with a request for a cold drink and two cookies, her eyes brighten and she arises from her chair with a surprising agility. And when the youngster fails to produce the required 15 cents, she just waves him on in mock disgust. "He'll be back," she says with a twinkle in her eye as she settles back down in the rocker. "He gets his allowance tomorrow."

Store fixtures: Seventy-four-year-old "Dude" Allen (**left**), a lifetime resident of Tarry, can be found sitting on the store counter all day every Saturday, according to Mrs. Thomas, while the store's old rocker (**above**) has been around almost as long as Dude Allen has.

THOMAS
GROCERY
your thirst
away
VICKS
COLDS
$500 REWARD
FARM BUREAU
MEMBER SERVICE

PRESERVING
THE PAST

Agricultural Museum, Scott, Arkansas.

Handmade brooms of all shapes and colors are the craft of pert Suzie Roll of Batesville. She exhibits at various arts and crafts shows throughout the state where, as she says, "I always make a clean sweep." She is not only a broom-maker but also holds almost every aeronautical rating, including an instructor ticket. Blue skies find her airborne in a red and white Piper Cub named "Coyote Duster."

The sounds of bluegrass music fill the air each spring at the Mountain View Folk Festival. The Stone County Courthouse square serves as a center of activities during the celebration, along with the Ozark Folk Center located a few miles away.

Footstompin' music to some may be a lullaby to others, as Today Robinson of Mountain View finds out with son Joshua.

Gene Waters of Austin, Arkansas (right), grinds sorghum at the old Sumler mill, located on highway 5 north of Cabot. After grinding, the juice from the sweet cane will be boiled down to form a thick brown syrup. "Sure tastes good in winter," says Waters. "Especially when there's snow on the ground."

An old marble-counter drugstore in Grady, Arkansas, still serves the best ice cream in town.

CONSTRUCTED IN 1820 of hand-hewn logs, The Territorial Restoration housed the meetings of the General Assembly before Arkansas became a state and entertained such notable figures as Davy Crockett, Sam Houston and Washington Irving. Now completely restored, the collection of old homes and buildings serves as a center for art displays, Rackensack folk concerts and craft festivals, complete with gingerbread and hot mulled cider served by mop-hatted Holly McDade (**right**).

T HE ARKANSAS STATE CAPITOL is the only state capitol with the same floor plan as the U.S. Capitol. After ground-breaking ceremonies in 1899, construction was completed under the leadership of Governor George W. Donaghey, and the General Assembly first met under its roof in 1911. The greater part of the stone used in construction is marble quarried in Batesville, Arkansas, and the dome, towering 185 feet above the first floor, is covered in 24K gold leaf.

Tour guide Mary Engel of North Little Rock leads a group up marble stairs toward the Senate chamber (**right**). Tours are free of charge and are given from 8:00 a.m. to 4:00 p.m. Monday through Friday, and from 1:00 p.m. to 5:00 p.m. Saturday and Sunday.

Take a ride into the past

THE SCOTT & BEARSKIN LAKE RAILROAD is an operational rail museum located in Scott, Arkansas, nine miles east of North Little Rock, and run by the R. L. Dortch family. The four steam locomotives are part of the R. A. Grigsby collection, and all are operable. The number one engine, a Mogul 2-6-0, built by the Baldwin Locomotive Works in 1906, is currently the oldest wood-burner with a "cabbage-head" stack running in the U.S.

A boy's first ride on a steam locomotive can be a pretty exciting experience, as attested to by Donnie Owen of Conway (**below**).

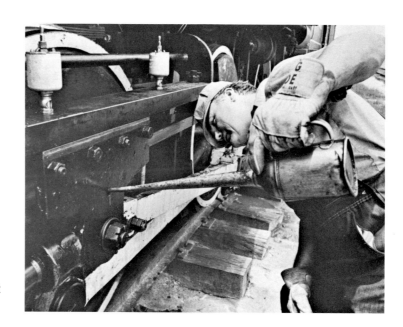

Mr. R. L. Dortch makes it go at Scott, Arkansas.

Monuments to the past

HANDCRAFTED DOVETAIL JOINTS (**left**) attest to days past in Newton County, while a popular soft drink selling for a nickel reflects pre-inflationary prices in Eureka Springs, (**above**), a resort community savoring a turn-of-the-century look. A pioneer grave will not be forgotten in a recently restored cemetery in Old Washington Historic State Park, Washington, Arkansas.

EXPLORING THE BUFFALO RIVER

Flowing free, the Buffalo River winds its way through 132 miles of towering water-stained bluffs and wooded hillsides in north central Arkansas. In the early 1960's, the River's future looked grim as the Army Corps of Engineers proposed the construction of two dams along its length. However, after a ten-year battle led by organizations such as the Ozark Society that generated vast public sentiment for preservation of the stream, the dam proposals were defeated, and in 1972 Congress passed the act authorizing the Park Service to establish a national river.

Near the headwaters of the river, between Boxley and Ponca, thickly forested Lost Valley State Park (**left**) offers exploring hikers an Indian cave large enough to build a house in, a natural bridge, an underground waterfall, and in the spring, a sprinkling of dogwood blossoms.

Further downstream, below Mt. Hersey, a canoeist explores the "Bat House" (**right**).

Morning fog blankets his campsite as early riser Jay Cromwell
of Pine Bluff reaches for the coffee pot.

Big Bluff - The High and Low of it.
Soaring upward 525 feet, "Big Bluff" earns its name by being the highest of the many stone cliffs lining the Buffalo. During spring thaws, giant icicles are melted loose from the rock face and come crashing down with a thunderous roar. A hiker (**left**) watches a small herd of horses cross the River far below.

River ghosts

With the discovery of zinc in 1880, Rush, Arkansas, became a bustling boom town of more than 2000 people, supported by several area mines. However, because the ore was scattered, mining operations slackened, and after a brief flurry of activity during World War I, Rush was abandoned.

Jimmy Alford and young out-of-state visitor Jerry Murphy check out a crumbling store (**left**), while the old mill (**right** and **above**) stands in silent testimony to the boom-and-bust mining activity half a century past.

The mouth of Rush Creek forms a scenic junction with the Buffalo, providing a favorite rest spot and swimming hole for canoeists.

Two pups in for a swim: When the fishermen are hot but the fishing is not, the only thing to do is take full advantage of a cold clear pool and plunge right in. Besides, later on in the afternoon an angler's luck is apt to change, as Jerry Murphy found out (**right** and **above**).

HEAVY PUBLIC USE exacts its toll each spring, when conditions for floating are usually deemed ideal. Up to 500 canoes are launched from Ponca on pretty weekends, and a normally peaceful river assumes a carnival atmosphere. Only through respect of a wilderness watershed's delicacy will the beauty of the Buffalo survive such heavy use. Arkansans are fortunate to have an abundance of other lesser-known waterways which, with public awareness, should help lighten the load of the Buffalo. Rivers such as the Kings, Spring, upper Ouachita, Caddo and Cadron Creek offer scenic floats, while the white water of Big Piney, the Mulberry and Bee Creek should be tackled only by experienced canoeists.

Two paddlers from Indiana check their orientation with veteran canoeist Cromwell (standing).

THIS IS

ARKANSAS ?

On the Goat Trail — Buffalo National River.

A street sign from another continent confronts the visitor at the Wiederkehr vineyards near Altus, Arkansas. Over half a million gallons of wine originate annually from the cellars of northwest Arkansas wine producers.

Out of control at Marble Falls - Arkansas' only ski resort.

Riding the wind, a glider soars over the North Little Rock airport. Soaring enthusiasts attempt to catch lift-giving "thermals" - heat convection currents from the ground which can carry their powerless craft upwards several thousand feet.

Summit! — Pinnacle Mountain: No special equipment is needed for an assault on the Pinnacle Mountain trail, just a sturdy pair of hiking shoes and hearty lungs. From the peak, a few miles west of Little Rock, a panoramic view of Lake Maumelle and the surrounding area can be literally breathtaking.

"DON'T CALL US FLATLANDERS!" grinned Joe Spradley, as he and fellow climber Mark Schmidt snapped on their gear for a climb up an overhanging rock face west of Pinnacle Mountain. Together they have amassed 17 years of climbing experience throughout the country, including a snow and ice "seminar" on Washington's Mount Rainier, and an ascent of Mount Orizaba in Mexico, the third highest peak on the North American continent. The two outdoorsmen conduct classes in technical rock climbing in Little Rock, aptly termed Rock I and Rock II in reference to their basic and intermediate courses.

Millions of years in the making and still growing. Stalagmites rise spectacularly in Blanchard Springs Caverns, one of the most beautiful living caves in North America, located near Mountain View.

Eyeing the camera: A zebra at the Little Rock Zoo provides the perfect subject for black and white photography (**above**), while tenseness shows in the face of a driver (**right**) as he awaits the start of formula V competition at the annual Grand Prairie Grand Prix near Stuttgart (**following page**).

"To soar over city" read the newspaper headline. However, when its earthly bonds were cut during a fourth of July celebration in Pine Bluff, a gusty wind swept the hot air balloon in a beeline route for the city limits, where it was safely recovered from a field.

Wingtips overlapping and afterburners ablaze, the U.S. Air Force Thunderbirds fly high during a demonstration at Blytheville Air Force Base.

Helping energize
the heartbeat of a state

WITH THE CONSTRUCTION OF ARKANSAS NUCLEAR ONE near Russellville, (**left**), Arkansas became the first state in the southwest with a nuclear-fueled electric generating station. The picture of health in North Little Rock (**below**), Melanie Mernah's life is affected in a different way by nuclear energy - her heart is governed by an atomic-powered pacemaker.

The day it
snowed -
North Little Rock

APPENDIX

Sources of Information about Arkansas

Persons interested in obtaining more information about
Arkansas can begin by contacting the sources listed below.

Department of Higher Education
    National Old Line Building
    Little Rock, Ark. 72201
    AC501-371-1441

Game and Fish Commission
    Capitol Grounds
    Little Rock, Ark. 72201
    AC501-371-1025

History Commission
    First State Capitol
    Markham and Center
    Little Rock, Ark. 72201
    AC501-371-2141

Hot Springs Chamber of Commerce
    Convention Center
    Hot Springs, Ark. 71901
    AC501-321-1700

Industrial Development Commission
    State Capitol
    Little Rock, Ark. 72201
    AC501-371-1121

Little Rock Chamber of Commerce
    1 Spring Building
    Little Rock, Ark.72201
    AC501-374-4871

Little Rock Public Library
    Reference Department
    7th and Louisiana
    Little Rock, Ark. 72201
    AC501-374-7546

North Little Rock Chamber of Commerce
    601 Main
    North Little Rock, Ark. 72114
    AC501-375-7294

Office of Arkansas State Arts and Humanities
    First State Capitol
    Little Rock, Ark. 72201
    AC501-371-2539

The Ozark Society
    Box 2914
    Little Rock, Ark. 72203

Parks and Tourism Department
    State Capitol
    Room 149
    Little Rock, Ark. 72201
    AC501-371-1511

Secretary of State
    State Capitol
    Little Rock, Ark. 72201
    AC501-374-1628

State Chamber of Commerce
    Wallace Building
    Markham and Main
    Little Rock, Ark. 72201
    AC501-374-9225

U.S. Department of Agriculture
    Cooperative Extension Service
    1201 McAlmont
    Little Rock, Ark. 72202
    AC501-376-6301